For a free color catalog describing Gareth Stevens Publishing's list of high-quality books and multimedia programs, call 1-800-542-2595 (USA) or 1-800-461-9120 (Canada). Gareth Stevens Publishing's Fax: (414) 332-3567.

The editor would like to extend thanks to Randall Farchmin, science instructor, Milwaukee Area Technical College, Milwaukee, Wisconsin, for his kind and professional help with the information in this book.

Library of Congress Cataloging-in-Publication Data

Casanellas, Antonio.
    [Transportes. English]
    Great discoveries and inventions that improved transportation /
by Antonio Casanellas; illustrated by Ali Garousi.
        p. cm. — (Great discoveries and inventions)
    Includes bibliographical references and index.
    Summary: Describes the evolution of land, sea, and air transportation including high-speed trains, submarines, and supersonic airplanes; includes instructions for science experiments relating to these vehicles.
    ISBN 0-8368-2587-X (lib. bdg.)
    1. Motor vehicles—Juvenile literature. 2. Transportation—Juvenile literature. [1. Motor vehicles. 2. Transportation.] I. Garousi, Ali, ill. II. Title. III. Series.
TL147.C35   2000
629.2—dc21   99-053259

First published in North America in 2000 by
Gareth Stevens Publishing
A World Almanac Education Group Company
330 West Olive Street, Suite 100
Milwaukee, WI 53212 USA

This U.S. edition © 2000 by Gareth Stevens, Inc. Original edition © 1999 by Ediciones Lema, S.L., Barcelona, Spain. Translated from the Spanish by Michael Stephen Roberts. Photographic composition and photo mechanics: Novasis, S.A.L., Barcelona (Spain). Additional end matter © 2000 by Gareth Stevens, Inc.

Printed in the United States of America

1 2 3 4 5 6 7 8 9 04 03 02 01 00

Gareth Stevens Publishing
A WORLD ALMANAC EDUCATION GROUP COMPANY

Trains

Trains have greatly improved over the years in order to compete with other forms of transportation, such as cars, buses, and airplanes.

Design engineers continually try to increase the speed of trains. The French high-speed train, Train à Grande Vitesse, or TGV, reaches speeds of more than 320 miles (515 kilometers) per hour without passengers on board. With passengers, the train can travel at 249 miles (400 km) per hour. Electric current powers the TGV, and computers control its routes. High-speed trains travel on rails that are farther apart than normal so that the trains can make turns safely.

Increased speed also increases the pressure on the rails. Therefore, high-speed trains in Japan and Germany use electromagnets to "float" on the track. These magnets lift the train about 0.4 inch (10 millimeters) above the rail.

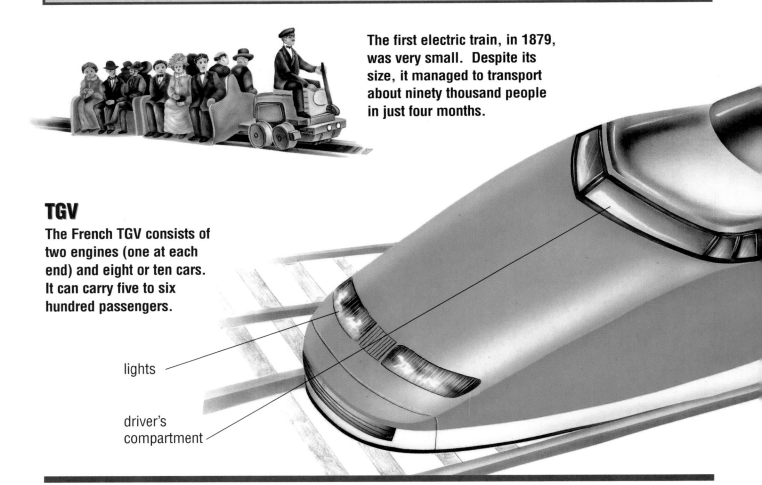

The first electric train, in 1879, was very small. Despite its size, it managed to transport about ninety thousand people in just four months.

TGV

The French TGV consists of two engines (one at each end) and eight or ten cars. It can carry five to six hundred passengers.

lights

driver's compartment

HOW DO ELECTRIC TRAINS WORK?

Electric trains are powered by electricity drawn through overhead pantographs, or trolley poles. The current of the cables above is very high, up to 15,000 volts, but transformers can reduce this. Many trains have an engine at each end, so they can travel in both directions.

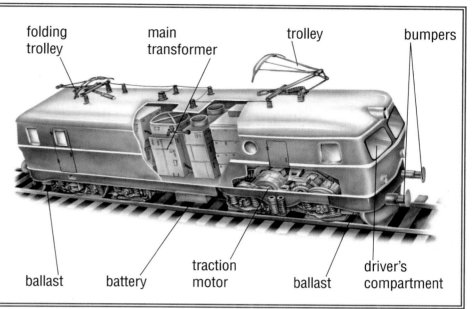

folding trolley

main transformer

trolley

bumpers

ballast

battery

traction motor

ballast

driver's compartment

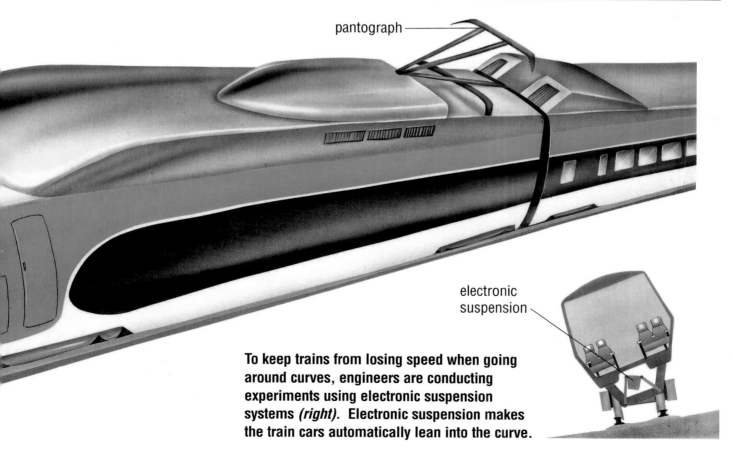

pantograph

electronic suspension

To keep trains from losing speed when going around curves, engineers are conducting experiments using electronic suspension systems *(right)*. Electronic suspension makes the train cars automatically lean into the curve.

Motorcycles

The first motorcycles, designed in the nineteenth century, were bicycles with an engine attached. Some of the earliest motorcycles were powered by steam engines. The people most often credited with the invention of the motorcycle are Germans Nikolaus A. Otto and Gottlieb Daimler. These inventors could never have imagined that, in a little over a century, motorcycles would become so advanced and popular. Today, motorcycles are available in a variety of sizes and engine powers. They are powered by either a two-stroke or four-stroke engine. Generally, single-cylinder motorcycles use a two-stroke engine. Motorcycles with a more than 200 cubic centimeter cylinder capacity require a four-stroke engine. Motorcycles are the perfect solution for short journeys, which are getting increasingly more expensive because of the high price of gasoline. In addition, motorcycles do not pollute the air as much as cars do. An added bonus is the freedom the motorcyclist feels traveling through the scenic countryside.

LARGE-CYLINDER MOTORCYCLE

Some of today's motorcycles can travel faster than cars.

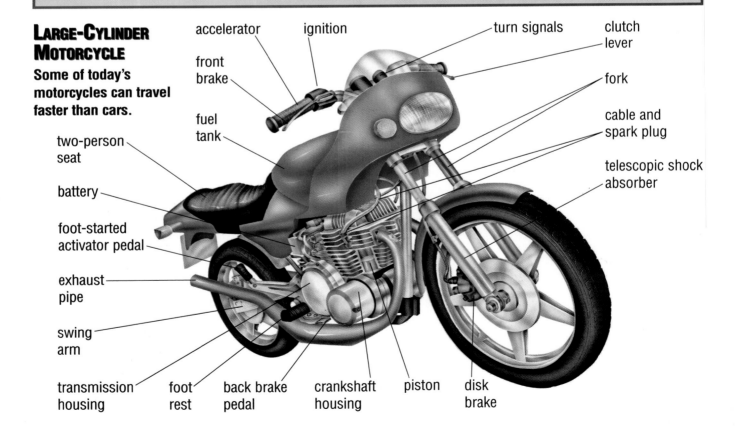

accelerator, ignition, turn signals, clutch lever, front brake, fork, fuel tank, cable and spark plug, two-person seat, telescopic shock absorber, battery, foot-started activator pedal, exhaust pipe, swing arm, transmission housing, foot rest, back brake pedal, crankshaft housing, piston, disk brake

THE TWO-STROKE ENGINE

The majority of small motorcycles operate with a two-stroke engine. The fuel is a mixture of gasoline and oil.

A. First stroke:
  1. Fuel and air enter the cylinder as the piston goes down.
  2. The piston drives the fuel and air into the combustion chamber via the delivery tube.
  3. The rising piston compresses the fuel.

B. Second stroke:
  4. A spark from the spark plug causes a small explosion that drives the piston down.
  5. The returning piston forces out exhaust gases. A chain or belt transmits the motion to the back wheel.

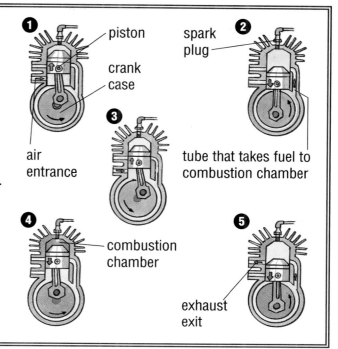

In 1885, the first motorcycle *(left)* was equipped with an internal combustion engine attached between the two wheels.

Large-cylinder racing motorcycles *(right)* are very aerodynamic.

Subways

Have you ever traveled on a subway? It is a very fast and comfortable means of transportation. The underground train developed similarly to the regular train. The first city to have a subway system was London, in 1863. Boston was the first city in the United States to have a subway, in 1897. Subway trains were originally powered by steam, but the coal smoke caused pollution. Subway trains are now driven by electricity.

The subway system is an ideal solution to the problems of traffic congestion and pollution in large cities. It efficiently transports large numbers of people through tunnels built underground.

The elevated railroad (sometimes called the el) is a type of rapid-transit system found in some cities. The trains run on tracks built above street level, making them less expensive to construct than a subway. Electricity powers el trains.

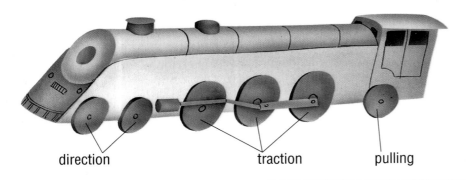

direction   traction   pulling

The first subway trains were powered by steam engines that had special wheels, each of which had a function — direction, traction, and pulling.

THE STREETCAR

The streetcar is another means of urban transportation. Streetcars travel along rails built into city streets. At the beginning of the twentieth century, streetcars were very popular. Today, they still exist in some cities, such as San Francisco in California, but they aren't as popular as they once were. Many people prefer faster methods of transportation, such as the subway. Mass transit of any kind reduces pollution in cities.

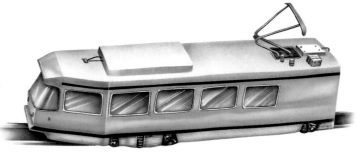

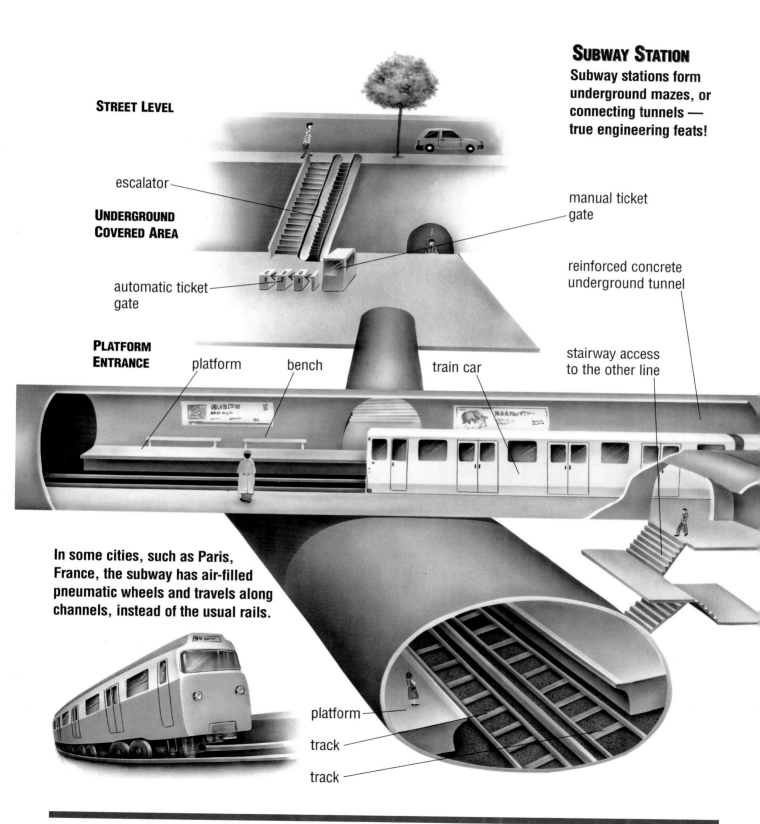

SUBWAY STATION
Subway stations form underground mazes, or connecting tunnels — true engineering feats!

STREET LEVEL

escalator

UNDERGROUND COVERED AREA

manual ticket gate

automatic ticket gate

reinforced concrete underground tunnel

PLATFORM ENTRANCE

platform   bench   train car

stairway access to the other line

In some cities, such as Paris, France, the subway has air-filled pneumatic wheels and travels along channels, instead of the usual rails.

platform

track

track

Specialized Trains

In 1829, a steam engine designed by George and Robert Stephenson pulled thirty-eight train carriages at a speed of 15 miles (24 km) per hour. That was a big achievement for the time. Little by little in the nineteenth century, the railway became the most popular means of transportation. It had one drawback, however. It could not climb steep hillsides. Twentieth-century designers set out to discover a solution for this problem and found it in the rack-and-pinion system and the funicular, or cable, system. Trains with these systems could travel up very steep hills. However, they could not go very fast.

The aerial cable car is another means of transporting people and goods up and down steep hills. Each car hangs from cables in the air, rather than traveling along tracks on the ground. The cables slide along by means of pulleys located in two separate towers. The suspended cars travel back and forth between the towers.

THE DIESEL ENGINE

A great technological leap in the history of railway transportation was made when the diesel engine replaced the steam engine. Diesel locomotives used an internal diesel combustion engine. They were more efficient than steam engines and did not pollute as much. The diesel engine produced electricity, which powered an electric motor that drove the train. A diesel engine always operated at the most efficient speed possible. With more and more advanced technology, today's modern electric engines replaced the diesel engines.

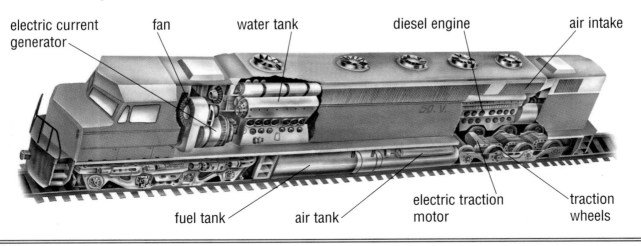

electric current generator · fan · water tank · diesel engine · air intake · fuel tank · air tank · electric traction motor · traction wheels

FUNICULAR

A funicular *(below)* is made up of two cars that travel via a cable that passes through a pulley. When one car goes up the hill, the other goes down the hill. They cross at a junction.

cogged track

upper drive wheel station

upper car

crossing junction

RACK RAILWAY

A wheel beneath the train fits into a cogged track between the rails *(above)*. This wheel moves the train uphill.

lower car

pulling cables

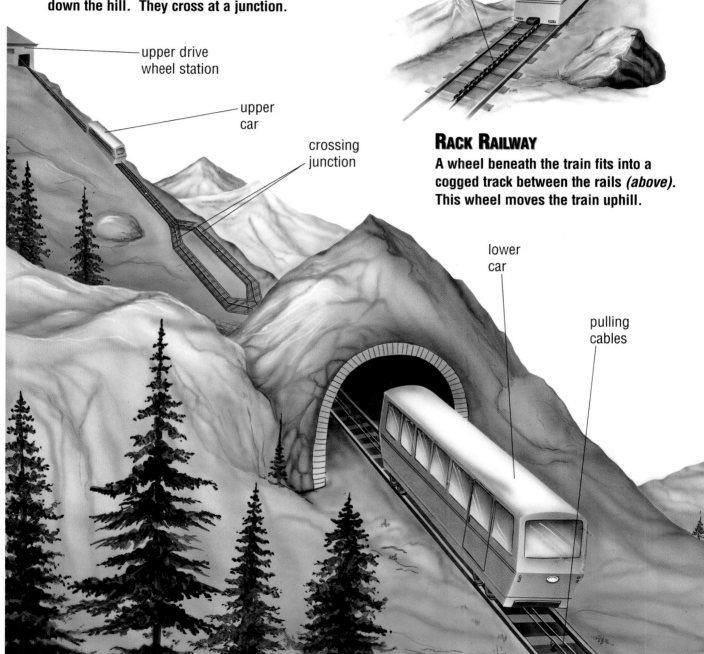

Submarines

The first craft to travel under water was invented by Cornelius Drebbel in England in 1620. The idea intrigued people of that time and in later centuries, but the submarine was not successful until the twentieth century.

The best known underwater vessel is the naval submarine, which usually carries torpedoes and missiles. It can measure more than 558 feet (170 meters) in length. On the surface of the water, submarines are powered by diesel engines. When submerged, they are propelled by electric batteries and motors. Some submarines are nuclear powered. They travel hundreds of miles (kilometers) without having to carry fuel. In 1948, Swiss scientist Auguste Piccard invented the bathyscaphe, which is much smaller than a submarine and can reach depths of 35,800 feet (10,912 m). The bathyscaphe explores the sea, undertaking deep ocean research. It is also used in repairing underwater cables and pipes.

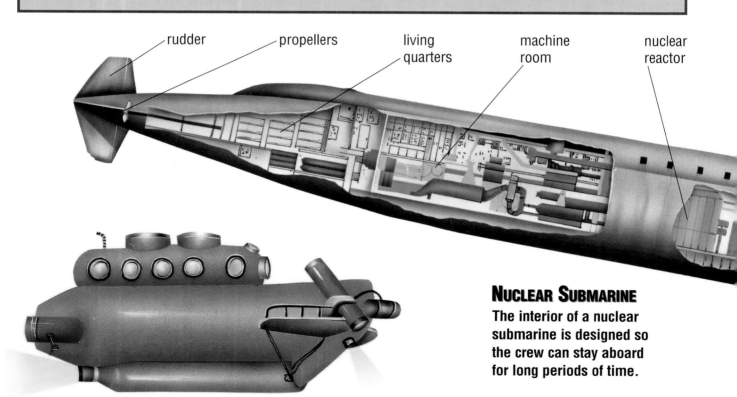

rudder   propellers   living quarters   machine room   nuclear reactor

NUCLEAR SUBMARINE
The interior of a nuclear submarine is designed so the crew can stay aboard for long periods of time.

The bathyscaphe *(above)* was designed by Swiss scientist Auguste Piccard in 1948.

SHIPS OF ANCIENT GREECE

Any object can float if it is shaped to push aside, or displace, enough water to equal its own weight. This includes both wooden vessels and iron ships. The first ships were made of wood. Crews of men rowed ancient Greek warships in time to a certain rhythm. On windy days, a large sail helped the ship move forward. The bow, or front, carried a large ram to strike enemy ships and sink them.

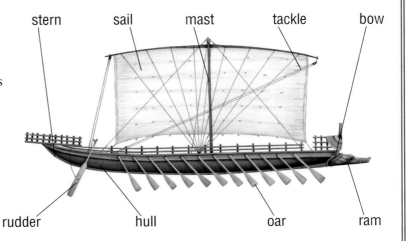

stern · sail · mast · tackle · bow · rudder · hull · oar · ram

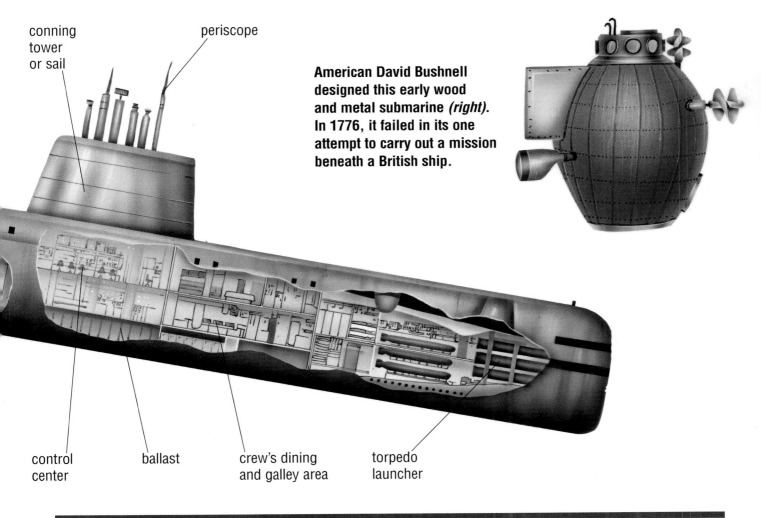

American David Bushnell designed this early wood and metal submarine *(right)*. In 1776, it failed in its one attempt to carry out a mission beneath a British ship.

conning tower or sail · periscope · control center · ballast · crew's dining and galley area · torpedo launcher

Sailing Vessels

Throughout history, people have sailed the seas for different reasons. The first cargo vessels were small sailing ships that hugged the coastline. Later, large ships were developed for ocean voyages. The best ship of its time for exploration was the caravel. The caravel originated in Portugal. It was a wooden vessel that carried lateen (triangular) sails and square sails. Square sails could sail before the wind. Lateen sails could use winds that blew at an angle to the ship. Steamships have now replaced sailing vessels. Today, only small sailboats use wind for power. Modern sailboats are mainly for pleasure outings and sporting competitions.

THE CARAVEL

Explorers Christopher Columbus and Ferdinand Magellan sailed the oceans in caravels. These ships were moved by the force of the wind. Caravels were larger and lighter than other ships of the period. They easily cut through the waves, which enabled them to travel faster than the other types of ships.

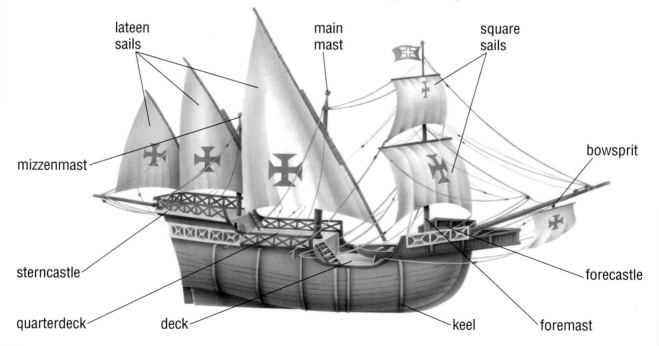

mast

genoa sail
or jib

bow

mainsail

port
hull

boom

stern

central
hull

starboard
hull

The trimaran *(above)* is a modern sailboat used for sporting competitions and pleasure trips.

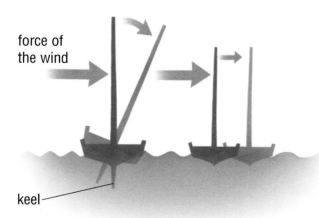

force of
the wind

keel

STAYING UPRIGHT

The keel stops a boat from being blown sideways by the wind. A strong gust of wind is blowing the boat with a keel *(far left)*. That boat tips but stays in one place. However, the boat without a keel *(left)* is being blown along across the water.

Ocean Liners

Ocean liners are huge vessels that are very much like floating modern cities. Powered by steam, they are descendants of the old paddle steamers.

French physicist Denis Papin discovered that steam could turn a paddle wheel and propel a ship. In 1769, Scottish engineer and inventor James Watt improved the steam engine. An engine built by Watt powered the first commercially successful steamboat. It was the *Clermont*, built in 1807 by an American, Robert Fulton, and launched in New York harbor.

For decades, ocean liners transported passengers and cargo on voyages to nearly anywhere in the world. Because airlines now move people and goods so fast, the ocean liner as a means of transportation is currently less desirable. However, vacation cruises have become popular.

The first ocean liners crossed the North Atlantic, uniting Europe with America. This ocean liner, the *Crown Princess,* was launched in 1990.

HOW DID PADDLE STEAMERS WORK?

Five hundred years ago, oarsmen rowed large ships across the seas. Italian scientist, artist, and inventor Leonardo da Vinci, who lived from 1452 to 1519, designed a ship that did not need oarsmen. His design featured a ship with large paddle wheels operated manually by a crank. At the beginning of the nineteenth century, the first commercially successful paddleboat propelled by steam was finally afloat. In 1807, the *Clermont*, designed by Robert Fulton, sailed down the Hudson River in New York. The illustration *(right)* shows a section of this type of boat. Modern ocean liners have powerful engines that drive metal propellers to move the ships.

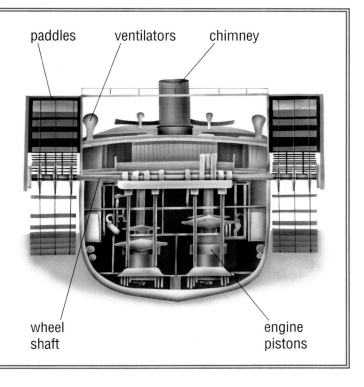

paddles   ventilators   chimney

wheel shaft   engine pistons

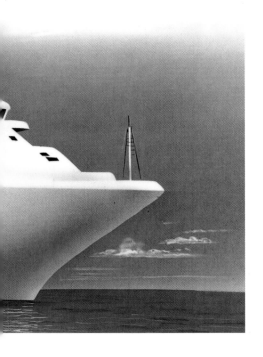

This paddle-propelled boat *(above)* is from the fifteenth century. The enormous wheel was turned by a man who walked inside it.

Supersonic Airplanes

In the 1940s, airplanes were driven by propellers turned by internal combustion engines. Once the planes reached the maximum speed possible using propellers, a faster system was desired. The jet engine eventually replaced the propeller engine. This jet engine moved an airplane forward by expelling gases backward. Over time, jet engines gradually reached higher and higher speeds. In 1947, American pilot Chuck Yeager dared to fly faster than the speed of sound at Mach 1.06, or about 700 miles (1,126 km) per hour. From then on, new types of airplanes have been developed, mainly for military use. In 1976, the Concorde, a civilian aircraft and the first supersonic airplane (SST), made its first transatlantic flight. The plane was a joint project between Great Britain and France. The Concorde flies at Mach 2.04, twice the speed of sound — about 1,453 miles (2,338 km) per hour. Despite its advantages, the Concorde has not been as successful as was hoped, due to high operating costs — three times more than those of conventional airplanes.

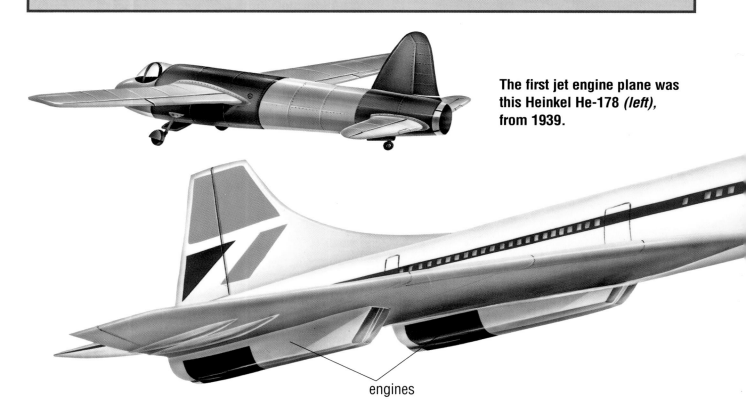

The first jet engine plane was this Heinkel He-178 *(left)*, from 1939.

engines

THE JET ENGINE

Jet engine planes, like the combat plane in this illustration, revolutionized the aeronautics industry. Jet engines led to aerodynamic design changes, with smaller, more angled wings for planes. The different types of jet engines all work in the same way. Air enters the chamber and is compressed by the first turbine. Afterward, fuel is injected. When the fuel is mixed with air, it ignites, and then expands. The gas produced is pushed out backward from the plane, propelling the plane forward and powering the second turbine, which turns the compressor turbofans.

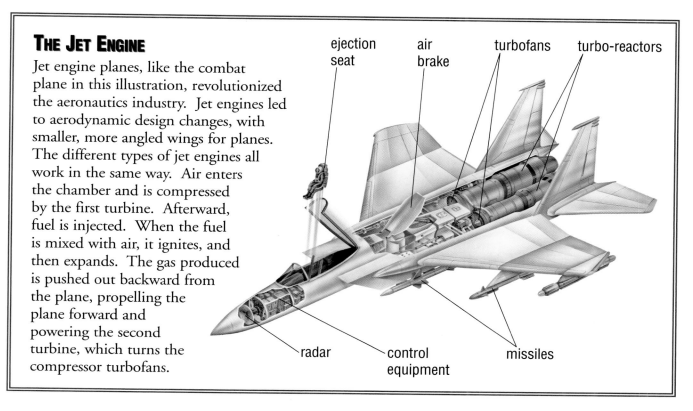

ejection seat · air brake · turbofans · turbo-reactors · radar · control equipment · missiles

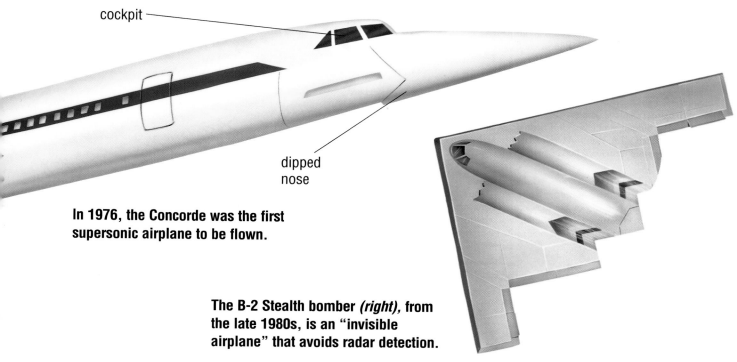

cockpit · dipped nose

In 1976, the Concorde was the first supersonic airplane to be flown.

The B-2 Stealth bomber *(right),* from the late 1980s, is an "invisible airplane" that avoids radar detection.

Turbo-propeller Airplanes

To fly in heavier-than-air machines is one of the greatest achievements humans have made. In order for planes to fly, the force of gravity has to be overcome. A great deal of observation and technological discovery went into the invention of the first flying machine. On December 17, 1903, in Kitty Hawk, North Carolina, two brothers, Wilbur and Orville Wright, flew for the first time. Their plane was the self-propelled *Flyer I,* commonly called *Kitty Hawk.* It was a heavier-than-air craft with a gasoline engine attached to it. In 1907, the Wright brothers contracted to build a two-person plane for the U.S. Army. This plane traveled 125 miles (200 km) at a time. Soon after, commercial aviation was born. Passenger planes attracted previous train and car travelers. Still, some people wanted to fly and ship cargo for short distances. Today, modern turbo-propeller airplanes meet that demand. These are small planes with jet-powered propellers. They fill people's needs while using less fuel than jet planes. Turbo-propeller planes are also used for traffic observation and fire control.

TURBO-PROPELLER
The turbo-propeller engine uses the energy released by a gas turbine to obtain jet propulsion.

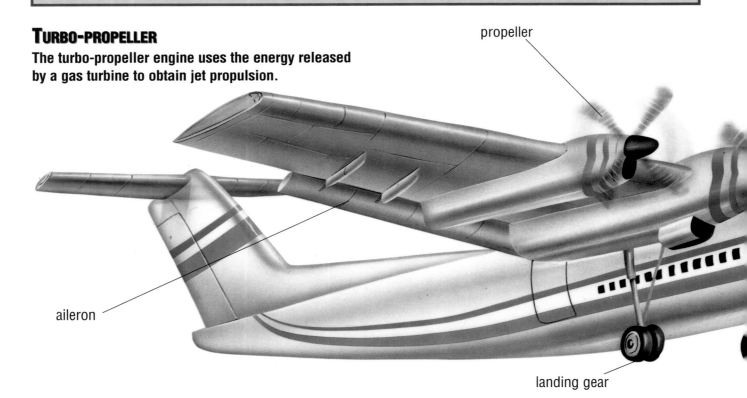

propeller

aileron

landing gear

How does a turbo-propeller work?

The Wright brothers equipped their airplane with a rudder and wings with curved surfaces. Today, airplanes have rudders and ailerons, as shown in the illustration *(right)*. Turbo-propellers work by using a combination of a propeller and a jet engine. Air enters at the engine's front and is compressed by a turbine. Fuel is then injected. This ignites, causing the movement of the turbine and the propeller.

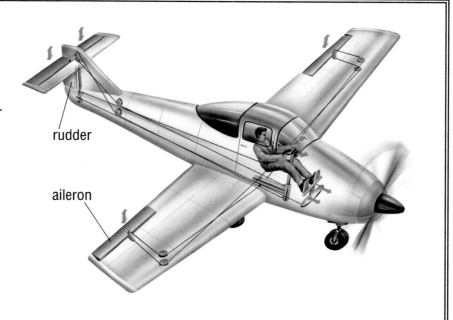

rudder

aileron

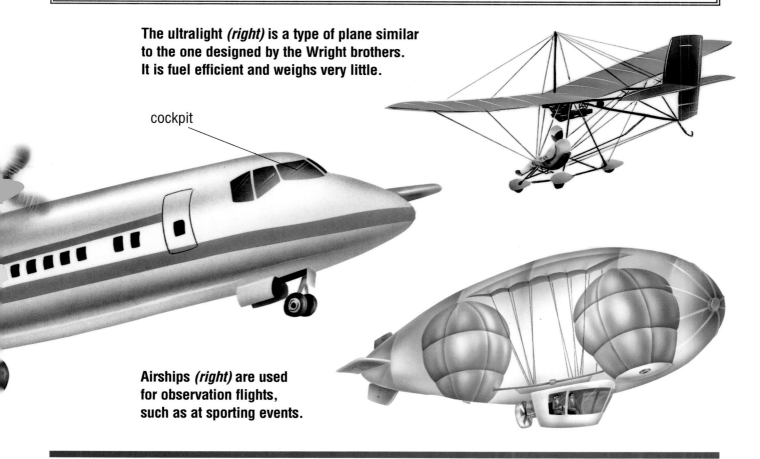

The ultralight *(right)* is a type of plane similar to the one designed by the Wright brothers. It is fuel efficient and weighs very little.

cockpit

Airships *(right)* are used for observation flights, such as at sporting events.

Hovercraft

In the seventeenth century, English scientist Sir Isaac Newton discovered that the forces of friction cause a body in motion to stop. In other words, a moving object slows down due to friction. Modern vehicles are built to reduce friction in order to obtain high speeds. Clear examples of this can be seen in the designs of cars, motorcycles, and airplanes. To minimize friction caused by air, they are aerodynamic, or streamlined with round edges and smooth lines. Not many boats are able to reach great speeds, though, because they are so big and must travel through water. The Hovercraft, or air-cushion vehicle, however, can reach speeds on the water of up to 75 miles (120 km) per hour. The Hovercraft rides over water and unobstructed land on top of an immense cushion of air. It is propelled by large fans. The modern Hovercraft was based on the 1950s work of English electronics engineer Sir Christopher Cockerell.

The Hovercraft *(above)* can travel across water and beaches.

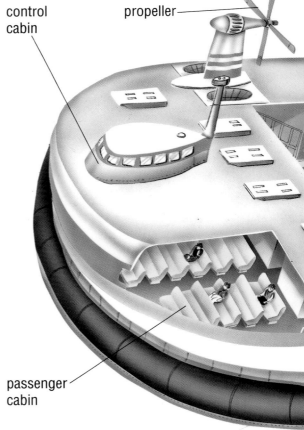

control cabin

propeller

passenger cabin

HOW THE HOVERCRAFT WORKS

Powerful fans on the deck of the Hovercraft blow air downward. This air is then drawn in through an opening in the craft and compressed. The compressed air is then blown to both sides of the vehicle and pushed inward, underneath the hull, or outside edge. This creates a cushion of air that raises the Hovercraft a few inches (centimeters) off the ground and allows it to move across any flat surface. The four large fans on the deck propel the boat.

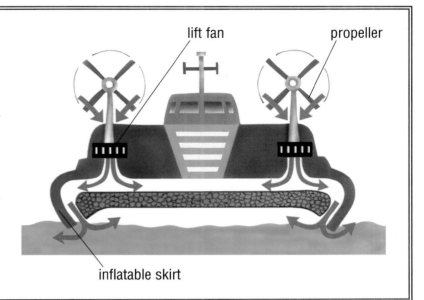

lift fan

propeller

inflatable skirt

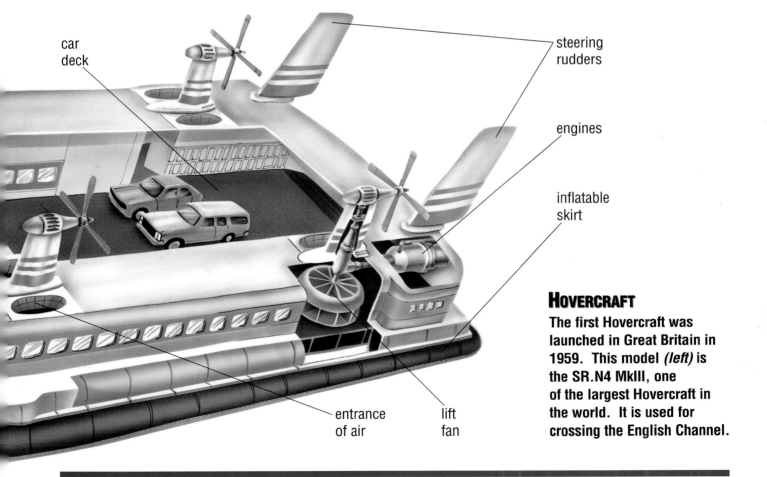

car deck

steering rudders

engines

inflatable skirt

entrance of air

lift fan

HOVERCRAFT

The first Hovercraft was launched in Great Britain in 1959. This model *(left)* is the SR.N4 MkIII, one of the largest Hovercraft in the world. It is used for crossing the English Channel.

Friction

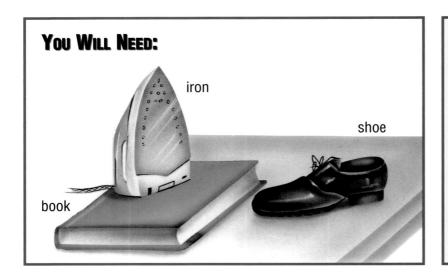

iron

shoe

book

The amount of friction that is produced depends on the surfaces in contact and the weight of the object to be moved. The friction between two objects is greatest just before one begins to move. Frictional resistance can be calculated mathematically. Overcoming friction is important for boats and airplanes. The following project will show differences in frictional resistance.

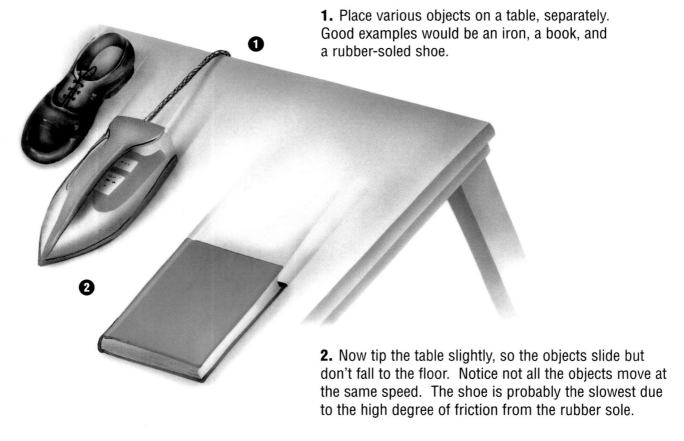

1. Place various objects on a table, separately. Good examples would be an iron, a book, and a rubber-soled shoe.

2. Now tip the table slightly, so the objects slide but don't fall to the floor. Notice not all the objects move at the same speed. The shoe is probably the slowest due to the high degree of friction from the rubber sole.

Reducing Friction

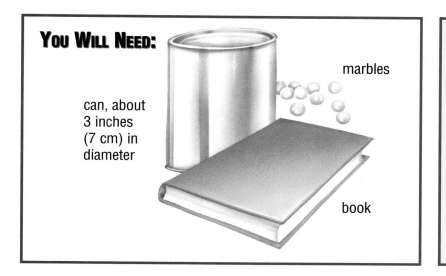

can, about 3 inches (7 cm) in diameter

marbles

book

Friction is caused by irregularities or roughness in surfaces that are in contact, and it prevents these surfaces from moving against one another smoothly and evenly. To reduce unwanted friction between objects, bearings are often used. The most common of all the bearings is the ball bearing.
To see the effect of ball bearings for yourself, do the project below.

1. Place a book on the top of a tin can. Turn the book back and forth with your hand *(as shown)*.

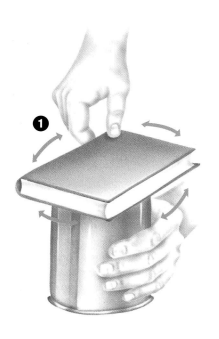

2. Now place some marbles on top of the can. They act as ball bearings.

3. Put the book on top of the marbles. Now turn the book back and forth. It moves much more easily than before.

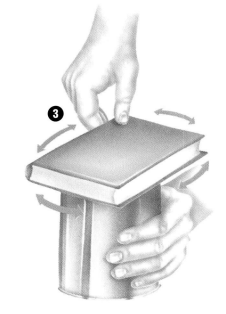

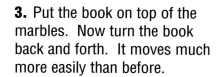

Archimedes' Principle

YOU WILL NEED:

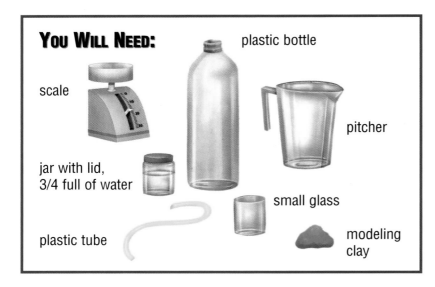

scale

plastic bottle

pitcher

jar with lid,
3/4 full of water

small glass

plastic tube

modeling clay

Do you know why boats float? In the third century B.C., the Greek mathematician and inventor Archimedes discovered that when any object is put into water, it pushes the level of the water up. He stated the principle that any object floating on or sinking into a liquid is floated upward by a force equal to the weight of the liquid pushed aside, or displaced. Archimedes' Principle is easily tested with the following project.

1. Carefully cut off the top of a plastic bottle. Make a small hole, and fit the plastic tube through it *(as shown).* Ask an adult to help.

2. Secure the tube using the modeling clay *(as shown).*

Next, weigh the small empty glass.

3. Fill the plastic bottle with water to just below the hole covered with modeling clay.

4. Place the empty glass next to the bottle. Place the other end of the tube inside the glass *(as shown)*. Now carefully put the small jar of water with the lid fastened into the bottle. The jar will push a certain amount of water out of the bottle, sending it down the tube into the glass.

5. Take the jar of water out of the bottle and weigh it.

6. Now weigh the glass that contains the water collected from the bottle. From this weight, subtract the weight of the glass itself when it was empty. The result is the weight of the displaced water. It should be the same as the weight of the jar of water that you submerged — Archimedes' principle in action.

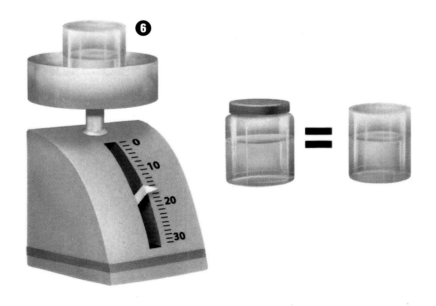

Wind Power

YOU WILL NEED:

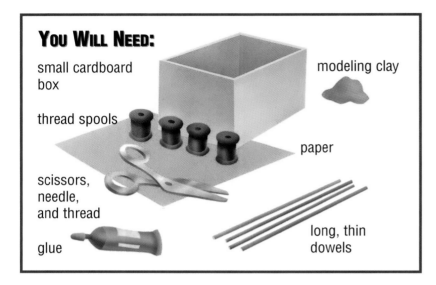

small cardboard box

thread spools

scissors, needle, and thread

glue

modeling clay

paper

long, thin dowels

For centuries, before the invention of steam engines, sails acted as "engines" for the ships that navigated the seas, carrying cargo or exploring the unknown. Various types of sails and different ways of rigging and handling them were developed to enable ships to sail under widely varying conditions and to different places. To experiment with the force that moved the ships of ancient times, do the following project.

1. Ask an adult to make four small holes, two on each side near the bottom of the box, with the scissors. These are for axles.

2. Next, ask the adult to use the scissors to make four slits in the box *(as shown)* for the mast dowel.

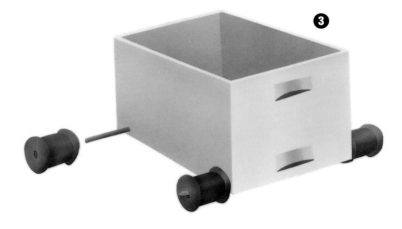

3. Slide the dowels into the holes *(as shown)*, and place a thread spool on each of the ends. Secure the spools in place with modeling clay.

4. Using a piece of paper and two dowels, make a sail. Curl the ends of the paper around the dowels *(as shown)*, and glue them in place.

5. Loop two pieces of thread, and use them to attach the dowels of the sail tightly to the dowel that is the mast. To do this, make small holes in the paper.

6. Now insert the mast through the two slits on the box *(as shown).* Steady it in place.

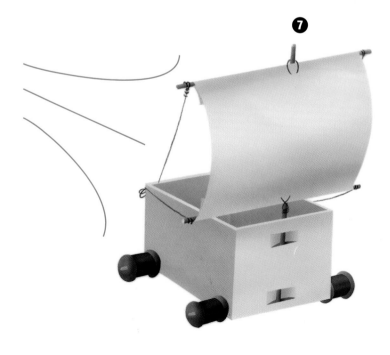

7. With thread, attach the two dowels of the sail to the back corners of the cart so that the sail does not move. Blow onto the center of the back of the sail, and watch how wind powered ships of the past.

Aerodynamic Design

YOU WILL NEED:

modeling clay

tall, clear container

watch

scale

Aerodynamic design uses shapes that go through the air more easily than others. An airplane must have an aerodynamic design so that its body experiences as little air resistance as possible. The same principle of aerodynamics applies to water resistance — it is called hydrodynamics. Ships are designed to move through water with the least resistance. This project tests the hydrodynamics of different shapes.

1. Cut the modeling clay into pieces of similar weight. Mold them into different shapes — a cube, an oval, a ball, a cone, and so on.

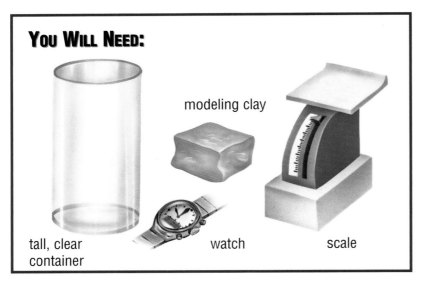

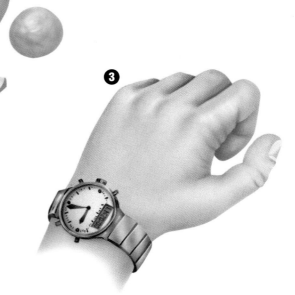

2. Fill the container with water. Prepare to time how long each piece of clay takes to reach the bottom of the container.

3. Drop the pieces of clay into the water, one at a time. Those that drop the most quickly have the most hydrodynamic shapes.

Ailerons

An airplane in flight uses three control surfaces for maneuvering. The pilot moves these flaps into position. In the tail are elevators, which are movable flaps that can make a plane climb or dive. The rudder in the tail turns a plane right or left on a level. Movable wing flaps, called ailerons, bank the plane, rolling it right or left. Do this project to see how an airplane turns by using ailerons.

1. Have an adult help you make a paper airplane like the one in the illustration *(below)*. Throw it, and watch how it flies without turning right or left.

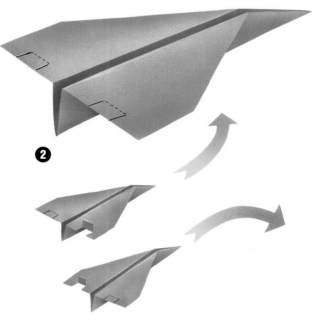

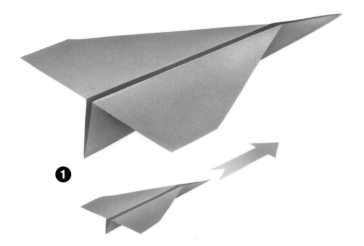

2. Now, cut a tab at the end of each wing *(above)* for the ailerons. Raise the tab on the right. The airplane should turn to the left when you throw it. Next, raise the tab on the left. The plane should turn to the right when you throw it.

Glossary

aerodynamics: the science of the force and speed with which air flows past an object in motion.

aeronautics: the science of flight and flying aircraft.

aileron: a movable, hinged part at the back edge of an airplane wing.

Archimedes's principle: the scientific law that states that when a solid object is immersed in, or set in, a liquid, it is held up in the liquid by a force equal to the weight of the liquid that has been pushed aside, or displaced, by the object.

bathyscaphe: a submersible sea vessel, built to withstand extreme water pressure, that is used for deep-sea exploration.

caravel: a small fifteenth- and sixteenth-century sailing ship with three or four masts that carried mostly lateen sails.

combustion: the burning of fuel in an engine.

diesel engine: an internal-combustion device in which air is compressed to a temperature high enough to ignite fuel that is injected into a cylinder where combustion and expansion move a piston.

electromagnet: a core of material, such as iron, surrounded by a coil of wire through which an electric current is passed, magnetizing the core.

forecastle: the upper deck of a ship in front of the foremast.

friction: the resistance of two objects moving against each other.

funicular: a cable railway, usually in mountainous regions. Counterbalances move one car up and another down.

hydrodynamics: the science of the force and speed with which liquids move past solid objects immersed in the liquids.

keel: the main timber, or wood piece, running along the center of the bottom of a boat or ship. It often extends below the boat or ship into the water to prevent the vessel from being blown sideways.

lateen sail: a large triangular sail hanging from a long slanting pole, or yard, that is supported by a straight up, vertical mast. The lateen sail uses winds blowing toward the sides of a ship.

piston: a short, solid metal piece that fits inside a cylinder and moves up and down, transmitting the engine's power.

pneumatic: working through air pressure on rubber or metal.

pulley: a small wheel that has grooved rims and contains a rope or chain. Power is transmitted through the rope or chain.

rack railway: a train that uses a wheel beneath it to move itself along a cogged track between the rails.

rudder: a flat structure attached to a vessel's end for the purpose of steering it.

streetcars: electrically powered cars, similar to trains, that run along tracks embedded in city streets.

subway: a system of trains that runs through tunnels beneath a city.

trimaran: a sailboat that has three hulls, which increase its stability in the ocean.

trolley: a system of poles that directs electric current from overhead cables to the engine of a train. Trolleys are also called pantographs.

turbine: a rotary engine activated by a current of water, steam, or air.

turbo-propeller: a type of airplane in which a jet engine runs a turbine that spins the propellers. The propellers and jet exhaust power the airplane.

More Books to Read

Across America on an Emigrant Train. Jim Murphy (Clarion)

Cars, Bikes, Trains, and Other Land Machines. How It Works (series). Ian Graham (Kingfisher)

Extreme Machines Under the Sea. David and Patricia Armentrout (Rourke)

Fantastic Transport Machines. Chris Oxlade and David Salariya (Franklin Watts)

How Do Big Ships Float? Ask Isaac Asimov (series). Isaac Asimov (Gareth Stevens)

Planes. Francesca Baines (Franklin Watts)

Planes, Gliders, Helicopters, and Other Flying Machines. How It Works (series). Terry Jennings (Kingfisher)

Record Breakers (series). (Gareth Stevens)

See and Explore Library: Trains and Railroads. Sidney Herbert Wood (DK Publishing)

Ship. David Macauley (Houghton Mifflin)

Stagecoach: The Ride of the Century. Richard Mansir (Charlesbridge)

Transportation: Automobiles to Zeppelins. June English (Scholastic)

Videos to Watch

Air Force One: A History. (Moonbeam)

Blue Angels: Those Amazing Jets: For Kids. (Library Video)

Ferryboats. (Outerbank Productions)

Stealth Jets. (Simitar Entertainment)

Steam Across America. (Questar)

There Goes a Boat. (Kimbo Educational)

There Goes a Motorcycle. (Kimbo Educational)

The Wright Brothers: Birth of Aviation. (Clearvue/eav, Inc.)

Traveling in Style: Trains, Riverboats, and Planes. (Library Video)

Web Sites to Visit

www.bicyclemuseum.com/

www.bonus.com/bonus/ *(Choose explore, America, Flying Wright Brothers.)*

www.neumedia.net/~cassrr/

www.historychannel.com
(Keyword: public transportation)

www.yahooligans.com/Science_and_Nature/ Machines

Some web sites stay current longer than others. For further web sites, use your search engines to locate the following topics: *airplanes, boats, Concorde, Hovercraft, motorcycles, Sir Isaac Newton, trains, transportation,* and *Wright Brothers.*

Index